Emily DeBaere

9/10/80

# MICHELANGELO

*Elizabeth Elias Kaufman*

CASTLE BOOKS
A Division of
BOOK SALES, INC.
110 Enterprise Avenue
Secaucus, N.J. 07094

ISBN: 0-89009-356-3

# CONTENTS

# COLOR ILLUSTRATIONS

# MICHELANGELO

Michelangelo, painter, sculptor, architect — his name is synonymous with great art. He belongs to that select group of creators whose art is timeless. More than five centuries after his death, student artists still pore over his works, marveling at his ability. His works are as breathtaking today as the day they were finished.

Michelangelo's work belongs to a relatively brief period known as the High Renaissance. It is a curious period in that it produced only a handful of masters, and just as few minor artists. In order to better understand the High Renaissance, it is best to begin with the Renaissance.

# HIS TIMES

The word "renaissance" means rebirth. The period known as the Renaissance has also been called the Age of Discovery and the Revival of Learning. Whatever title is given, the Renaissance represents a breath of fresh air, removing the last vestiges of the Middle Ages; allowing European culture to go forward, and at the same time, to rediscover her past.

The beginning of the fifteenth century saw an enormous upheaval in the world of art, starting first in Italy. The Renaissance began in Italy for a number of reasons. Geographically, Italy was a crossroads for trade, allowing new ideas to enter. There were economic and political changes occurring in the area. Italy was home to a tremendous amount of classical Greek and Roman art. Although all of these factors contributed, the most important factor in the development of the Renaissance in Italy was a change in philosophy.

The Middle Ages had been dominated by the Church and its philosophy. Art was considered to be a rather mechanical thing; the artist was simply arranging his materials in a more or less preordained way. The fifteenth century witnessed a change in the relative importance of religious and secular elements. The dominance of the Church gave way to an increased interest in material values. During the Middle Ages, life was important only because it led to life eternal. Now men saw the importance of life on earth. Philosophers attempted to reconcile classical philosophy and Christianity. This helped move art and the artist out of the crafts and into the realm of the liberal arts. The artist joined the scholar and poet as a creator.

There were three overlapping characteristics of the Renaissance: classicism, humanism, and individualism. The rediscovery of the classical past is evident in the profusion of Renaissance nudes, totally absent in medieval art. The translation of religious themes into natural terms — humanism, added life to the symbolic art of the Middle Ages. For the first time abstractions were seen as they influenced man. The individualism of the Renaissance is best demonstrated in the number of famous Renaissance artists. Each was allowed to create his own concept. His art was no longer judged by one set of standards. He was free to interpret the world as he saw it.

The term, High Renaissance, has been given to a short period at the end of the fifteenth century and beginning of the sixteenth century. The true masters of the period were Bramante, Leonardo di Vinci, Michelangelo, Raphael, Titian, and Giorgionne. The power and prestige of these artists was so strong that it was close to three hundred years before art scholars "rediscovered" the art of the early Renaissance.

The High Renaissance is often referred to as the climax of, or the logical conclusion, to the Renaissance. In many respects this is true; in other ways, this brief period represents a departure from the Renaissance.

The art of the High Renaissance is a reaction to the excesses that preceded it. The three characteristics of the Renaissance: classicism, humanism, and individualism were all present in the High Renaissance, but there were significant changes.

The humanism of the Renaissance became less superficial as art assumed a more idealized form. The artist tried to find ideas and ideals that had universal meaning and appeal. Thus, the Madonna became a woman, capable of a woman's suffering. At the same time, the classical style moved away from generalizations. This was accomplished by introducing strain and tension. The concept of individualism, so important in Renaissance art, underwent an even more significant change. The High Renaissance viewed the artist as a genius. His ability was due to "divine" inspiration. This Neo-platonistic philosophy had a number of consequences. It prodded the artist to undertake enormously large and complicated projects. It also encouraged wealthy men to sponsor the artist and to commission his art.

The artistic characteristics of the High Renaissance are easy to observe. Works created during this period are often very large — the *David* (plate 5) towers above the viewer. The idealized type is in some respects similar to Greek art. Notice, for example, the idealized face of the Madonna in the *Pietà* (plate 3). In contrast to Greek art, however, High Renaissance art is filled with strain and tension. It is easy to feel the power of the *Rebellious Slave* (plate 31) as he tries to break his bonds. The final characteristic of the High Renaissance, a sense of drama, is perhaps the most important characteristic. It is the drama, the visual excitement, that seems to elevate the art of this period. The anger of *Moses* (plate 30) is so strong that it speaks to the observer. There is nothing soothing about this art. It demands that the viewer participate.

The masters of this period used their intellect as well as their artistic skill. They changed the geometry of their art to gain greater plasticity. They used the fifteenth century developments in anatomy and perspective, but they used them in an almost offhand manner.

It is no wonder that the High Renaissance lasted for such a short period of time. The genius of the masters could not be transmitted to their followers. In fact, the High Renaissance died when the masters did. But during this brief time, they created some of the most famous, enduring, and beloved art works of all time.

# HIS LIFE

Michelangelo was born on the sixth of March in 1475. He was the second son of Lodovico di Lionardo Buonarroti Simoni and Francesca di Neri. His father was a member of an old and noble Florentine family that had become impoverished. Michelangelo was born in Caprese, a town in Tuscany, where his father was serving a six month term as the mayor of the region.

Little more than a month after his birth, his father's term of office expired, and the family returned to Florence. Michelangelo was placed in the care of a wet nurse in Settignano, a few miles from Florence. The area had many stone quarries, and like most of the men in the town, the foster father was a stonecutter.

The impact of this man's profession on

the young Michelangelo cannot be stressed enough. The first ten years of his life were spent in Settignano where stonecutting was a way of life. It is possible that Michelangelo's first play toys were a hammer and chisel. For the rest of his life, he had an affinity for these tools.

In 1485, at the age of ten, Michelangelo was brought back to Florence. His mother had died in 1481, and his father had remarried. He lived with them, his four brothers, and an uncle. For the next few years, he went to school. By all accounts, it was not a happy experience.

Three years later, in 1488, he became friendly with a young painter who was apprenticed to the Ghirlandaio brothers. In April of that same year, at the age of thirteen, Michelangelo convinced his father to allow him to become an apprentice in the same workshop. His father was not happy about it; he felt it was not a proper occupation for the son of such a noble family.

The Ghirlandaio brothers were primarily fresco painters. It was in their studio that Michelangelo learned the techniques he would later apply in the Sistine Chapel. During the first year of his apprenticeship, he proved to be more interested in the art of past masters such as Giotto, Masaccio, and Donatello than in the work being done in the studio. He also spent a great deal of time examining the ancient Greek and Roman art in the city.

Although they had hired him for a three year apprenticeship, the Ghirlandaio brothers allowed him to leave at the end of the first year to enter Bertoldo di Giovanni's school for sculptors located in the garden of the Medici palace. In 1490, Michelangelo's work caught the eye of Lorenzo de' Medici who invited the fifteen-year-old boy to live as a guest in the palace. Michelangelo lived there until 1494.

His four year stay with the Medicis was crucial to his intellectual development. Although he could not help but be influenced by the cultural climate in Florence, the palace was home to the leading humanists of the times. Michelangelo sat in on, and perhaps participated in nightly philosophical discussions. The men and their philosophy seem to have inspired his *Madonna of the Stairs* (plate 1) and *Battle of the Centaurs* (plate 2).

It was during this period that Michelangelo studied anatomy by dissecting corpses. As a result of his study, he mastered the art of human anatomy. Throughout his career, his ability to pose the human figure was a trademark.

In 1494, Florence was overrun by the French army. Michelangelo fled to Bologna and Venice. He returned in 1495. Although he created a number of pieces on his return to Florence, none of them have survived.

A year later, in 1496, Michelangelo went to Rome where a collector commissioned several of his works. This same collector helped him obtain a commission from a French cardinal for the *Pietà* (plate 3) in St. Peter's Cathedral. Despite admiration for his work, he received no further commissions in Rome. In 1501, he again returned to Florence.

In Florence, he accepted a commission for fifteen statues for an altar in Siena. However, before this project was fairly begun, he started work on *David* (plate 5). This monumental work was completed in 1504.

In 1505, Michelangelo was called to Rome by Pope Julius II and given a gigantic commission for the Pope's tomb. He spent more than six months in the marble quarries at Carrara choosing the marble and supervising its cutting. But on his return to the city, he felt threatened by intrigue, and so he fled to Florence. The original commission was never finished, although several figures for it were completed. For years, Michelangelo tried to return to it. The fact that he was constantly being interrupted to assume other commissions is often given as the prime reason for the bitterness of his later life.

In 1508, Michelangelo returned to Rome,

summoned by Pope Julius II to paint the ceiling of the Sistine Chapel. He was desperately unhappy about accepting the commission, for he considered himself to be a sculptor, not a painter. He felt that the commission was a result of his enemies intriguing against him. For four years, he labored sixty-eight feet above the ground painting the ceiling.

The death of Pope Julius II in 1513 required a new contract for the tomb. There were to be several more changes in the contract, each new version reducing the size of the monument. An abbreviated version of the original commission was finished in 1542.

For twenty years after finishing the ceiling of the Sistine Chapel, Michelangelo worked in Florence. He designed and completed most of the work in the Medici Chapel, although he had to interrupt his work to act as a military engineer when Florence was attacked again. He left Florence in 1532, never to see it again.

In 1534, he was commissioned by Pope Paul III to do the altarpiece in the Sistine Chapel. *The Last Judgment* (plates 38-42) was finished in 1541. It suffered attacks for its many nudes. Michelangelo refused to change the work, so another artist was hired to clothe the nude figures.

For the next several years, his work was predominantly religious in nature, including the *Crucifixion of St. Peter* (plate 44). In 1558, he began work on a model for the dome of St. Peter's Cathedral. He never saw the finished dome. In 1565, Michelangelo died in Rome. He was buried in his beloved Florence.

Michelangelo's long career as an artist had several consistent themes. From birth to death, he was a sincere Christian. At the same time, he was a firm believer in the High Renaissance concept of the artist as a genius. He truly believed in the rightness of his art. For most of his life, Michelangelo was subject to violent changes in mood, to a certain degree of paranoia, and to a gloomy personality. It is somewhat ironic that this unhappy man's art has given the world so much pleasure.

# HIS WORKS

## PLATE 1

Michelangelo was sixteen years old when he created the *Madonna of the Stairs.* It is an interesting work in that it shows the influence of the early Renaissance while at the same time showing Michelangelo's concern with the human figure. Although the Virgin's form is not totally delineated, the shape of the nursing Christ is quite clear. Michelangelo has given Him a powerful upper torso and arm. His tutor at this time was Bertoldo who had been a pupil of Donatello. This marble relief is reminiscent of Donatello's work.

## PLATE 2

Another marble relief sculptured during Michelangelo's stay at the Medici Palace is his *Battle of the Centaurs.* The inspiration for this piece might have come from a Roman sarcophagus. The idea probably came from a leg-

end he learned from the humanists living in the palace. *Battle of the Centaurs* was created only one year after *Madonna of the Stairs* (plate 1), yet already his ability to handle the human body is obvious. Although many of the details are not clear, each figure shows the body in a different pose. The artist must have had a special fondness for this work. It is one of the few pieces he kept all his life.

## PLATES 3, 4

The *Pietà* in St. Peter's Cathedral is the culmination of Michelangelo's youthful period. He was only twenty-four years old when it was installed in the old St. Peter's. A "pietà" is any image of the Virgin holding the dead Christ. Thousands have been created, but such is the impact of this one piece of art, that even today, the word conjures up the image of this particular sculpture.

Michelangelo was commissioned to create it in 1498 by a French cardinal. At the time it was a novel sculptural idea in Italy. Part of the commission was a written guarantee that this would be the finest marble work in Italy.

The artist handled his tragic subject in a unique fashion. Before this, all pietàs showed the Virgin in a state of bereavement. However, Michelangelo has idealized the Virgin. She appears to be younger than her Son. Her sorrow shows most poignantly in her outstretched hand and in the heavy folds of her dress. The form of a pyramid was used to add to the solemnity of this compact sculpture.

This *Pietà* is an excellent example of Michelangelo's use of proportion to meet the needs of his art. He has made the adult male smaller than the Virgin. If the Virgin were to stand, she would be approximately seven feet tall, yet her head is no larger than her Son's. If the Christ were larger, or the Virgin smaller, He would appear to be too large, destroying the compactness and balance of the work. The balance of the piece is so right that the normal viewer is never aware of the altered proportions.

Of all his sculptures, this is probably the most highly polished. It is also the only sculpture Michelangelo signed with his correct name. The work has been damaged twice. Four fingers of the Virgin's left hand were broken off and replaced during the eighteenth century. The piece was damaged again during this century while on loan. Repairs have since been made.

## PLATE 5

Michelangelo's *David* is often considered to be the first statue of the High Renaissance. It was commissioned in 1501 when the artist was twenty-six years old. When it was finished in 1504, the entire city of Florence knew he had created a masterpiece.

The character of David had been sculpted before. In fact, Florence already had two David sculptures, one by Donatello, and one by Verrocchio. Michelangelo's *David* was startlingly different. First of all, in sheer size, it dwarfed the other two. (It also dwarfs the viewer.) This David's face is idealized. He is heavily muscled and has reached young manhood. Earlier versions were dainty boys, often wearing flowered hats.

Although this piece belongs to the High Renaissance, it still shows some characteristics of the earlier Renaissance. The position of the right wrist is identical to the wrist on an earlier sculpture by Donatello. The detailed anatomical work and the fixed glance of the eye also link this sculpture to the earlier period.

However, there is no doubt that the *David* belongs to the High Renaissance. In contrast to earlier sculptures of David, which show the hero as victorious and relaxed, this one is waiting for Goliath. There is a sense of strain and tension in the figure. The artist achieved this by lifting a shoulder, showing the tension in the neck muscles, and by giving the face a slightly angry cast. The head and right hand are exaggerated in size to add drama and emotion. Unlike earlier sculptures of the same character, this *David* really looks capable of defeating Goliath.

*David* was carved out of a huge block of white Carrara marble. The block had been the object of considerable interest by artists for several decades. An earlier sculptor had started work on it, but later abandoned it. The "giant" as the unflawed block was known, was considered quite a prize.

The city of Florence commissioned *David* and gave Michelangelo the "giant" from which to carve it. It was supposed to be placed high above ground on the Cathedral. However, when it was finished, the elders of the city realized that Michelangelo's *David* was a perfect symbol for the city itself. The Biblical David was not only a proud warrior, he was also a wise and just ruler. The spirit of the times was right for this *David*. A committee of about thirty artists, one of whom was Leonardo da Vinci, was formed to find a

9

proper place for it. They finally decided that the best spot for the statue would be in front of the Palazzo Vecchio. An earlier sculpture by Donatello was moved to make room for the **David**. Although the statue has been moved inside to the Accademia, a copy of the original still stands in front of the Palazzo Vecchio. During a turbulent period in Florence, the left arm was broken in three pieces by a bench, thrown from a window. The pieces were replaced in 1543.

Through the years, **David** has been the subject of considerable analysis. Some scholars claim Michelangelo was making a political statement about Florence — that the city should be strongly defended and wisely governed. Another group of scholars detect a religious statement. During the Middle Ages, the right side of the body was thought to be shielded by God; while the left side was open to evil. **David** gazes to the left, awaiting the approach of Goliath, a symbol of evil. A third group claims that Michelangelo, having recently returned from Rome with its many ancient statues, merely wanted to carve a huge nude figure. Whether the colossal work had a political, religious, or historical message, or no message at all is still not clear.

What is clear is the beauty of the statue. Although tense and grim with determination, **David** also has a sense of calm. This stationary action is a characteristic of Michelangelo's work.

## PLATE 6

In **Combat of Horsemen and Foot Soldiers**, Michelangelo's skill as a draftsman is apparent. The force of the drawing suggests the sounds of the battle.

## PLATE 7

The **Doni Madonna** is a tondo, a favorite form of art in Florence. A tondo is a circular piece of art similar to a large medallion.

Michelangelo did three of them at about the same time. They take their names from the family that commissioned them. This one is named for Angelo Doni. It is believed to have been commissioned in honor of his marriage.

The **Doni Madonna** is done in tempera on a wooden panel and is the only known surviving easel painting definitely attributable to Michelangelo. Because of the hard edges, the figures of the Holy Family look as if they have been carved rather than painted. The background (not pictured) could almost be a separate painting — there are five well-detailed nudes lolling behind the Holy Family.

Though this painting is not one of Michelangelo's better pieces, it does seem to have elements that appear later in the Sistine Chapel ceiling.

## PLATE 8

This tondo is known as the **Pitti Madonna** after Bartolommeo Pitti who commissioned it. In contrast to the **Doni Madonna** (plate 7), this is a marble relief. It does not appear to be completely finished. The work is sometimes known as the **Madonna with Baby and St. Giovannino**.

## PLATE 9

The section of the Sistine Chapel illustrated here (from the western part of the ceiling) gives a good overview of the entire ceiling. The chapel was built by Pope Julius II's uncle, Sixtus IV, for whom it is named. It is a long, fairly narrow room. The ceiling measures approximately 45 feet by 128 feet and is 68 feet from the floor. During the fifteenth century, murals had been painted on the walls by prominent artists. Before Michelangelo began, the ceiling was a pale blue punctuated by gold stars. When he finished, he had covered almost 5,800 square feet with more than 300 figures. That this was accomplished by one man, almost unaided, is unbelievable, yet true.

Michelangelo did not want to accept the Pope's commission to paint the ceiling of the Sistine Chapel. He felt that he was a sculptor, not a painter, and that his enemies had conspired against him to embarrass him. When the Pope insisted, Michelangelo reluctantly agreed. The work got off to a bad start. The original scaffolding was suspended from the ceiling. When it would have been removed, there would have been no way to cover or paint the holes it left in the ceiling. Another scaffolding had to be built. Michelangelo had trouble with the first actual fresco. The base had been incorrectly mixed. When it refused to dry and grew moldy, it had to be removed.

The original plan for the ceiling was based on twelve giant figures around the edges with decorations in the middle. After consulting with Pope Julius II, Michelangelo changed the design. The final plan called for nine main panels (four large ones alternating with five smaller ones), five sibyls, seven prophets, the ancestors of Christ in the spandrels, medallions, and nude youths. The whole unified by a painted architecture that both divides and unites the entire work.

The main panels down the center are scenes from the book of Genesis. They start with the creation of the world and end with a scene showing the drunkenness of Noah. These panels are usually thought of in three groups of three, representing the creation of the world, the creation of man, and man's sins. The section illustrated in this plate shows the first third, the creation of the world.

This portion was one of the last parts to be completed. Michelangelo started at the far end, over the entrance to the chapel with *The Great Flood* (plate 22). The last panel, *God Dividing the Light from the Darkness* is above the altar.

The figures look as much like sculptures as like paintings. They are extraordinarily expressive. As in his sculpture, Michelangelo used the human body to tell his stories. In the bottom right-hand corner of this portion sits the prophet *Jeremiah*. This melancholy figure appears to be a portrait of frustration and despair. It is interesting that *Jeremiah* is thought to be the artist's self-portrait.

Next to *Jeremiah* is one of the ancestors of Christ, *Salmon*. To her right is the *Persian Sibyl*, sitting with her face averted, her pen moving across the pages of her book. Above her are two of the many nudes (plates 12-16). Notice that they are supporting a medallion between them. In the center to the left is the panel of *God Dividing the Waters from the Earth* (plate 17). Above this panel is the prophet *Daniel*. It is believed that this part of the ceiling was damaged at one point and that *Daniel's* head and arm have been repainted. In the spandrel next to *Daniel* is another of Christ's ancestors, *Jesse*. In the upper right-hand corner is the *Libyan Sibyl*, her body turning, her arm muscles bulging under the weight of her book. Between *Jeremiah* and the *Libyan Sibyl* is the first of the main panels, *God Dividing the Light from the Darkness*. Finally, in the middle of this portion is *The Creation of the Sun, Moon, and Planets* (plates 10, 11), one of the four large main panels.

Throughout the ceiling, Michelangelo used cool, subdued tones. The paintings become lighter in color towards the center, thus highlighting the most important panels.

## PLATES 10, 11

*The Creation of the Sun, Moon, and Planets* is one of the four large main panels on the ceiling of the Sistine Chapel. Surrounded by cherubs, the Lord points in two directions. In this panel, He is represented as the Old Testament Jehovah — full of anger. The face of God has a sculptured feel. The sweep of the drapery around Him and the slant of His hair and beard give the impression He is moving at great speed.

## PLATES 12, 13, 14, 15, 16

The nude figures in plates 12 through 14 surround *The Creation of the Sun, Moon, and Planets* (plate 10). Plates 15 and 16 are the two nudes below *The Fall of Man* (plate 20). The ceiling of the Sistine Chapel has approximately twenty of these nude figures. They sit on heavy blocks at each corner of the main panels serving to unite the Genesis scenes. These athletic youths work in pairs to support the ribbons holding up the decorative medallions.

They are portrayed in different moods from sadness to joy, and from thoughtful to almost playful. In expressing these moods, Michelangelo has used a wide variety of poses. Some of the figures are in positions impossible for the human body to attain. Many of them are contorted enough to actually overlap the main panels. For example, the mass next to the sun in *The Creation of the Sun, Moon, and Planets* (plate 10) is actually the arm and part of the ribbon a nude is holding.

No one is quite certain what the significance of the nudes is. The moods can be seen as representing conditions of the human spirit. They could also collectively represent paganism. Whatever their meaning, they are marvels of sculptured painting.

## PLATE 17

This panel from the ceiling of the Sistine Chapel, *God Dividing the Waters from the Earth,* provides a sharp contrast to the *The Creation of the Sun, Moon, and Planets* (plates 10, 11). Here, God appears to be blessing the earth. Gone is the fire and brimstone, replaced by a kindly, understanding Divinity. The figure of God, borne aloft by three cherubs, seems to be moving in a gentle swirl. There are few hard angles; most of the composition is based on circles. This is a much softer, mellower piece than *The Creation of the Sun, Moon, and Planets*.

## PLATES 18, 19

*The Creation of Adam* occupies part of the center of the Sistine Chapel ceiling. Its prominent position and dramatically charged subject matter have made it one of Michelangelo's most famous works.

The artist chose not to portray Adam as alive, or the physical creation of Adam. Instead, he shows the viewer Adam, reclining on the earth, in the instant before the birth of his soul. There is so much electricity in the piece, that the observer can almost feel the Divine spark flow from one outstretched finger to the other.

Neither Adam nor God appears happy. Adam has a languid, almost sorrowful look on his face. The face of God shows His intensity and concentration.

Under the left arm of God is the unborn Eve. She too appears worried. Adam, although perfectly proportioned, appears to be quite heavy. This provides a good contrast with the figure of God sweeping across the sky.

## PLATES 20, 21

*The Fall of Man* is actually only the left half of a full panel on the ceiling of the Sistine Chapel. In this half, Adam and Eve receive the forbidden fruit from the serpent who is wound around the tree of knowledge. In the right half of the panel, they are forced out of the Garden of Eden by an angel with a sword. Part of the angel is visible in the upper right-hand corner of plate 20.

Adam stretches for the fruit, while Eve receives hers from the serpent. Adam's face has been turned away from the viewer, but Eve's face shows longing. Michelangelo's Garden of Eden is a rocky, barren place. The only vegetation appears to be the tree of good and evil. It is an interesting concept of Paradise, and says much about the man who created it.

## PLATES 22, 23

*The Great Flood* was the first of the Genesis scenes to be painted on the ceiling of the Sistine Chapel. The base for the fresco was not made properly. It never dried, grew moldy, and had to be scraped off and repainted.

The artist treated his subject sympathetically. He knew what it meant to flee in fear of his life. This panel is unique among the Genesis scenes for its multitude of figures. Its subject matter would have been difficult to illustrate with only a few figures as in the other main panels.

In the background of the piece, Noah and his family are seen on the ark. In the middle, a group of people have found a small boat. Several more are trying to climb aboard it. The angle of the boat indicates that the additional weight will cause it to overturn. Struggling up a steep incline, people are carrying household goods. Notice the woman who carries her possessions on top of her upturned table. To the right, a man carries a dead body. The detail in plate 23 shows the faces of the two figures on the left, one carrying the other. Michelangelo introduces a high wind during the flood. The streaming hair on the figure who is being carried and the bent tree on the left were all he needed to illustrate the wind.

## PLATE 24

The spandrel showing *David and Goliath* is located on the left-hand side in the corner over the door of the Sistine Chapel. This rendition is often compared with his sculpture of *David* (plate 5). The sculptured hero is awaiting Goliath. Here, Michelangelo depicts him in the midst of the battle, with his sword held high, ready to deliver the final blow.

## PLATE 25

On the right-hand side in the corner over the door of the Sistine Chapel ceiling is this spandrel of *Judith and Holofernes*. In contrast with the spandrel showing *David and Goliath* (plate 24), this one shows Judith and her handmaiden after the deed has been done. Judith is about to cover the severed head. The body lies beyond.

## PLATE 26

The *Cumaean Sibyl* is one of the least attractive subjects on the ceiling of the Sistine Chapel. Old, wrinkled, and frowning, she broods over her book. Looking over her shoulder are two soft and attractive cherubs. The *Cumaean Sibyl* is an interesting figure. Her heavily muscled legs and arms and her powerful shoulders are very masculine. The strength and youth of the arms do not seem to match the furrowed brow and sagging cheeks. Michelangelo has posed her in an incredibly contorted position, adding to the tension of the figure and deepening the gloom of the piece.

## PLATE 27

The detail of the *Delphic Sibyl* from the ceiling of the Sistine Chapel is a total contrast to the *Cumaean Sibyl* (plate 26). The *Delphic Sibyl* is young and attractive. Her head is erect and turned, as if towards a voice. She gazes with clear untroubled eyes. The mood of this sibyl is light and innocent. Unlike the *Cumaean Sibyl*, this sibyl does not carry the weight of the world on her shoulders.

## PLATE 28

This drawing, *Studies for the Crucified Haman*, was made for one of the spandrels on the ceiling of the Sistine Chapel. It is an excellent example of Michelangelo's ability to use perspective. Notice the way he deals with the arm closest to the viewer. The drawing also illustrates his ability to express emotions through the human form. The exposed neck muscles below Haman's upturned and tilted head show his agony.

## PLATE 29

In the drawing known as *Study for a Putto and Hand*, Michelangelo's preoccupation with poses is obvious. With only a few lines he shows the full musculature in various poses. The position of the hand was an important aspect in a number of Michelangelo's works. Here he was working on a hand holding an object. In the upper left-hand corner of this sheet, he was also working on part of an architectural design.

## PLATE 30

The sculpture of *Moses* was to have been part of the tomb of Pope Julius II. It is now in the church of San Pietro in Vincoli in Rome. Many scholars consider this piece to be among Michelangelo's finest sculptures. It is often compared with *David* (plate 5). However, *Moses* is a product of the mature artist. It is much more of a character study than the earlier work.

*Moses* sits holding the two tablets of the law. Like the *David, Moses* shows stationary action. With one leg drawn back, he is ready to stand. His face shows great anger. The hand in his lap shows repose, but the hand in the beard shows nervous or contemplative energy.

The detail work in this sculpture is extraordinary. The viewer can easily see the veins in his hands and arms. The hair and beard are very clearly delineated. Tremendous attention was given to the folds of drapery.

## PLATE 31

The sculpture known as the *Rebellious Slave* was intended for the tomb of Pope Julius II. However, the revised version of the tomb had no room for the statue. It is now in the Louvre in Paris.

There are several theories on the significance of these slave figures. The most elaborate theory states that the figures represent the liberal arts, once free, but after the Pope's death, returned to slavery.

In contrast to the *Dying Slave* (plate 32), the *Rebellious Slave* is still fighting his bonds, his powerful muscles straining against them.

## PLATE 32

Like the *Rebellious Slave* (plate 31), the sculpture of the *Dying Slave* was to have been part of Pope Julius II's tomb. The original plan called for a series of these figures, each in a different pose. This figure gains its poignancy from the face which shows the collapse of its will power. The tremendously powerful body is spent; its energies consumed in the struggle.

## PLATE 33

The drawing, *Sketch for a Resurrection*, illustrates Michelangelo's concern for the human form. The body of Christ is very clear, but the averted head is no more than a blur.

## PLATE 34

*Victory* might have been intended as part of the original version of the tomb of Pope Julius II. In that case, the sculpture would be a contrast for the slave figures (plates 31, 32). It is believed that after Michelangelo's death, the piece was worked on by other artists. It is a somewhat strange statue coming as it does after *Moses* (plate 30) and the slave figures.

## PLATE 35

The *Head Study for Leda* reveals something of Michelangelo's technique. Apparently unsatisfied with the angle of the nose, he drew another partial face with a more pleasing angle. Notice that in the second drawing, the eye has lashes.

## PLATE 36

This drawing of *The Resurrection* has a light, buoyant feel to it. Although Christ is presented as well-muscled, He has a lyrical quality. This is perhaps the most upbeat of all of Michelangelo's religious works.

## PLATE 37

The simplicity of *Young Woman's Head* is deceptive. The drawing shows a woman deep in thought. It also shows the artist's interest in detail. Even though it is only a sketch, he has given the woman an earring.

## PLATES 38, 39, 40, 41, 42

These details from *The Last Judgment* in the Sistine Chapel show a few examples of the multitude of characters found in the work. The painted surface is more than 2,000 square feet. The artist required five years to do the work, aided only by a man to grind his colors.

Michelangelo received the commission for *The Last Judgment* in 1534 from Pope Clement VII. Shortly after the commission was given, the Pope died. Pope Paul III, who succeeded him, wanted the work done. It was two more years before the painting actually began. In that time, windows and paintings were bricked over and a tilted wall was constructed, supposedly to protect the work from dust. The original base for the painting had been prepared for an oil painting. Michelangelo preferred to work in fresco; so the base had to be removed and a new one applied. More than twenty years after finishing the ceiling of the Sistine Chapel, Michelangelo began work on the wall over the chapel altar.

*The Last Judgment* has a somber, gloomy mood. The large figure of Christ looks stern. *Mary* (plate 38), who sits to His right, looks away from Him. The work is divided into three zones or areas. The first is the Heaven. Christ is surrounded by the Virgin, apostles, patriarchs, and martyrs. Even *St. Peter* (plate 39) with his key seems angry. The face that appears behind St. Peter (plate 40) shows fear of Christ's decision.

The second area or zone holds those who have been or are about to be judged. On the right are the damned; on the left, the elect. In the middle of this area, God's angels blow trumpets (plate 41) to announce His Judgment. To the right of the angels is the figure of a soul being dragged down into Hell by a demon (plate 42). The third area shows Hell with all its attendant horrors: demons, devils, tortured souls, and Minos, the prince of Hell.

Michelangelo's purpose was to shock the viewer and to cause him to reflect and repent his sins. Among those who were strongly affected by the work was Pope Paul III. Two men who made objections while Michelangelo was still working on the piece found themselves portrayed in *The Last Judgment* in an unflattering fashion. In addition, the flayed skin held by St. Bartholomew is thought to be the artist's self-portrait.

Much of what is seen today was not executed by Michelangelo. At different times, objections were raised to the profusion of nudes over the chapel altar. These nudes were covered by a succession of artists. The first to do so became known as "the breeches maker".

## PLATE 43

The sculpture of *Brutus* is believed to be only partially Michelangelo's work. It shows the man who betrayed and murdered Caesar in a favorable light. This is indicative of the way Michelangelo felt about tyrants.

## PLATE 44

Commissioned by Pope Paul III for his private chapel, *The Crucifixion of St. Peter* (along with its companion piece, *The Conversion of St. Paul*), represents the last stage of Michelangelo's paintings. *The Crucifixion of*

*St. Peter* was finished when he was seventy-five years old.

The detail shown in this plate appears in the top left-hand side of the work. The faces of the soldiers show fear, guilt, and uncertainty. The captain of the soldiers points towards St. Peter, but looks backs over his shoulder as if unsure what to do or say.

## PLATE 45

The *Florentine Pietà* was begun by Michelangelo in 1547. Before finishing the piece, he mutilated it and never touched it again. However, his servant saved it from total destruction by asking for it as a gift. Another artist worked on the Mary Magdalen to the left and polished part of the Christ figure. One of Christ's legs is missing. The mutilation is still very visible.

The male figure above Christ is Joseph. However, it is believed to be a self-portrait of the artist who originally wanted the sculpture placed on his tomb.

## PLATE 46

The sketch of *The Annunciation* was made at about the same time Michelangelo was working on the *Florentine Pietà* (plate 45) and other religious subjects. The face of the angel is a strange mixture of Michelangelo's styles. This was apparently a working sketch; the position of the Virgin's left arm was changed.

## PLATE 47

The *Crucifixion with the Virgin and St. John* illustrates the religious intensity of Michelangelo's later life. On the left, the Virgin stands in a pose of bereavement. Notice that although she has her arms crossed on her breast, at one time her right arm was by her side. St. John's head has also been altered. The cross itself is interesting. Instead of the usual **T** shape, Michelangelo forms the cross in the shape of a **Y**.

## PLATE 48

Begun in 1555, the *Rondanini Pietà* was never finished. Michelangelo was still working on it in 1564 when he died. This pietà is so different from the *Pietà* in St. Peter's (plates 3, 4), it almost looks as if they were done by different artists. The figures in this sculpture are elongated. They seem to have grown together through some sort of spiritual fusion. At this point in his life, Michelangelo was more interested in the spiritual and emotional content of his work than in realistically portraying beautiful bodies. There is very little of the High Renaissance in the *Rondanini Pietà*.

The sculpture is really only a fragment of the original work. It is believed that Michelangelo was dissatisfied with the original head of the Virgin, removed it, and carved another from the remaining marble. The statue was reworked several times. The legs of Christ and the right arm are all that are known to be left of the original version. Unfinished and abstract, the *Rondanini Pietà* was a very personal statement of Michelangelo's Christian spirit.

**Plate 1  Madonna of the Stairs,** c. 1491, marble relief, 22″ × 15¾″,
Casa Buonarroti, Florence

**Plate 2  Battle of the Centaurs,** c. 1492, marble relief, 33¼″ × 35⅝″,
Casa Buonarroti, Florence

**Plate 3 Pietà,** 1498-99, marble, 5′9″ high, St. Peter's Cathedral, Vatican, Rome     19

**Plate 4  Pietà,** detail — head of the Virgin

**Plate 5 David,** 1501-04, marble, 13′5″ high, Accademia, Florence

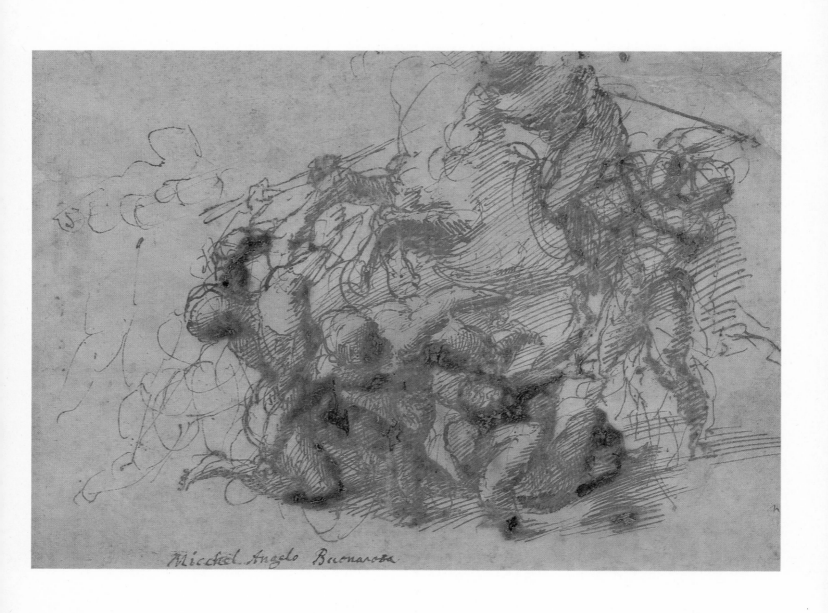

**Plate 6  Combat of Horsemen and Foot Soldiers,** 1504, pen drawing,
7″ × 9⅞″, Ashmolean Museum, Oxford

**Plate 7  Doni Madonna,** detail — Holy Family, c. 1504, tempera on wood,
diameter 47¼″, Uffizi, Florence

MICHELANGIOLO
Madonna con Bambino

**Plate 8 Pitti Madonna,** c. 1506, marble, diameter 33½″ , Bargello, Florence

**Plate 9  Sistine Chapel ceiling,** detail — western portion,
1511, fresco, Vatican, Rome

**Plate 10  The Creation of the Sun, Moon, and Planets,**
detail from Sistine Chapel ceiling

**Plate 11  The Creation of the Sun, Moon, and Planets,** detail — Jehovah's head, from Sistine Chapel ceiling

**Plate 12 Nude,** detail from Sistine Chapel ceiling

**Plate 13 Nude,** detail from Sistine Chapel ceiling 29

**Plate 14 Nude,** detail from Sistine Chapel ceiling

**Plate 15 Nude**, detail from Sistine Chapel ceiling 31

32       **Plate 16 Nude,** detail from Sistine Chapel ceiling

**Plate 17  God Dividing the Waters from the Earth,**
detail from Sistine Chapel ceiling

33

**Plate 18  The Creation of Adam,** detail from Sistine Chapel ceiling

**Plate 19 The Creation of Adam,** detail — Adam's head,
from Sistine Chapel ceiling                                        35

**Plate 20 The Fall of Man,** detail from Sistine Chapel ceiling

**Plate 21 The Fall of Man,** detail — Eve's head,
from Sistine Chapel ceiling

**Plate 22  The Great Flood,** detail from Sistine Chapel ceiling

**Plate 23  The Great Flood,** detail — two heads, from Sistine Chapel ceiling    39

**Plate 24  David and Goliath,** detail from Sistine Chapel ceiling

**Plate 25  Judith and Holofernes,** detail from Sistine Chapel ceiling        41

**Plate 26  Cumaean Sibyl,** detail from Sistine Chapel ceiling

**Plate 27  Delphic Sibyl,** detail — her head, from Sistine Chapel ceiling    43

**Plate 28  Studies for the Crucified Haman,** 1511, red chalk, 10″ × 7½″,
Teylersmuseum, Haarlem

**Plate 29  Study for a Putto and Hand,** 1511-13, red chalk and pen,
11¼″ × 7⅝″, Ashmolean Museum, Oxford                    45

46    **Plate 30 Moses,** 1513-16, marble, 8′4″ high, San Pietro in Vincoli, Rome

**Plate 31  Rebellious Slave**, 1513-16, marble, 7′⅛″ high, Louvre, Paris          47

**Plate 32 Dying Slave**, 1513-16, marble, 7′6½″ high, Louvre, Paris

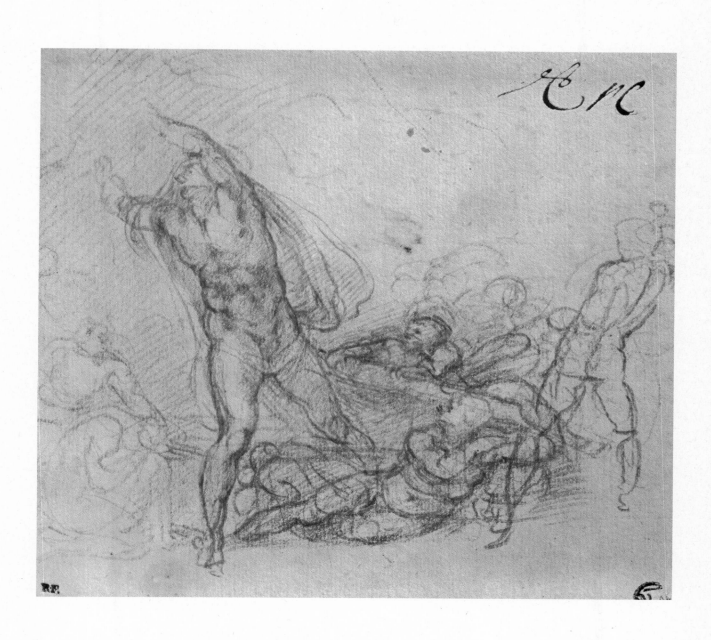

**Plate 33 Sketch for a Resurrection,** 1520-25, red chalk, 6⅛'' × 6¾'',  Louvre, Paris      49

**Plate 34  Victory**, 1527-28, marble, 8′6¾″ high, Palazzo Vecchio, Florence

**Plate 35  Head Study for Leda,** 1529-30, red chalk,
14″ × 10⅝″, Casa Buonarroti, Florence

**Plate 36  The Resurrection**, c. 1533, black chalk, 16″ × 10⅝″,
British Museum, London

**Plate 37  Young Woman's Head,** c. 1533, red chalk, 8″ × 6½″,
Ashmolean Museum, Oxford                                    53

**Plate 38 Last Judgment,** detail — Mary, 1537-41, fresco,
altar wall of Sistine Chapel, Vatican, Rome

**Plate 39 Last Judgment,** detail — St. Peter, from altar wall of Sistine Chapel

**Plate 40 Last Judgment,** detail — face behind St. Peter,
from altar wall of Sistine Chapel

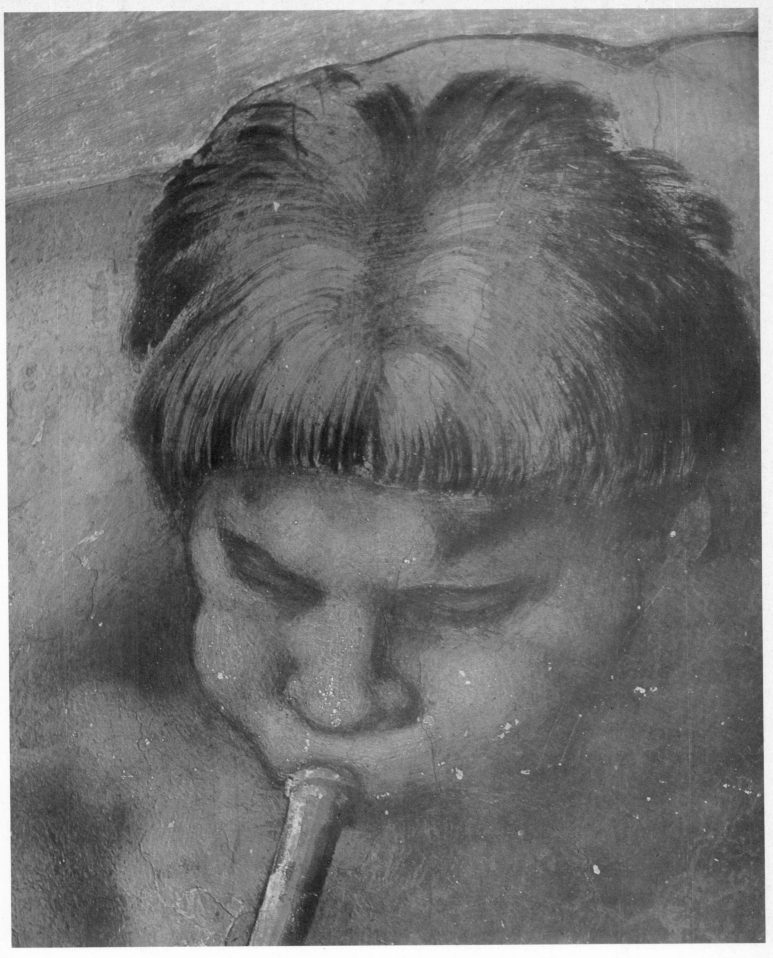

**Plate 41 Last Judgment,** detail — angel from altar wall of Sistine Chapel 57

**Plate 42 Last Judgment,** detail — demon, from altar wall of Sistine Chapel

**Plate 43  Brutus,** c. 1542, marble, 29⅛″ high, Bargello, Florence          59

**Plate 44 The Crucifixion of St. Peter,** detail — soldiers, 1545-50, fresco,
Pauline Chapel, Vatican, Rome

**Plate 45 Florentine Pietà**, 1547-55, marble, 7′8″ high, Cathedral, Florence      61

**Plate 46  The Annunciation,** 1550-60, black chalk, 11⅛″ × 7¾″,
British Museum, London

**Plate 47  Crucifixion with the Virgin and St. John**. 1550-56, black chalk with white pigment and gray wash, 16⅜″ × 11¼″, British Museum, London

**Plate 48  Rondanini Pietà,** 1555-64, marble, 6′3¾″ high, Castello Sforzesco, Milan